ST1CKER PUZZLES

FOR CREATIVE KIDS

Meet
··Emma and Ben··

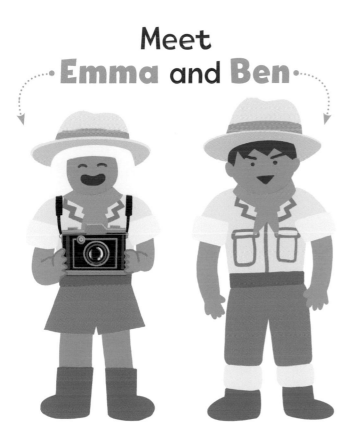

These explorers are on an exciting adventure gathering objects for their new collection. They will travel the world taking pictures with their camera. But their camera isn't ordinary—

it's extraordinary!

In fact, when they take a picture of an interesting item, it turns into a small object.

Join them on their journey, and help them collect special objects to add in their secret hideout!

Emma and Ben start their adventure in an orchard.

As they walk past the trees, they pluck a sweet, crunchy **apple** from a branch.

Ben takes a picture of it—and it turns into a small object!

▶ Use the puzzle stickers on page 25. When you finish, find the object's sticker on page 45 and place it in the secret hideout on page 23.

Next, Emma and Ben visit a bakery. They taste

a delicious slice of strawberry **cake**!

Click!

Emma snaps a picture, and the piece of cake

turns into a small object for their collection.

▶ Use the puzzle stickers on page 27. When you finish, find the object's sticker on page 45 and place it in the secret hideout on page 23.

The explorers are hungry and stop at a diner.

Ben takes a picture of

his **cheeseburger**.

It's one of his favorite meals. Yum!

▶ Use the puzzle stickers on page 29. When you finish, find the object's sticker on page 45 and place it in the secret hideout on page 23.

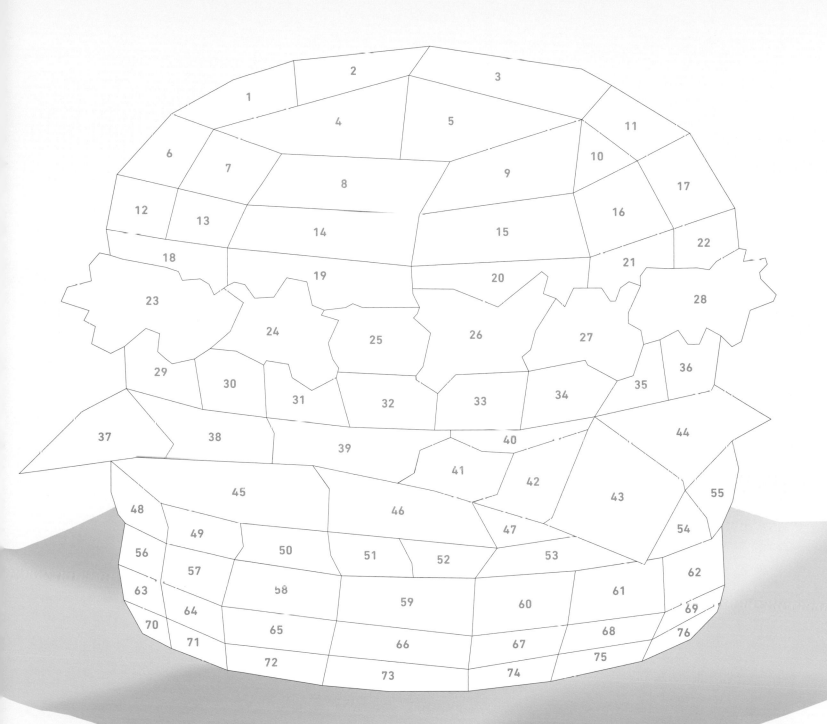

After traveling all day, Emma and Ben rest near a cuddly

new friend—a giant **panda**!

They take a quick nap, and then they're ready for

their next adventure. But before leaving,

they take a picture of the panda.

▶ Use the puzzle stickers on page 31. When you finish, find the object's sticker on page 45 and place it in the secret hideout on page 23.

It's a hot day, and the explorers cool off with a playful **elephant**.

They splash in a puddle while the elephant sprays them with water and trumpets with delight!

▶ Use the puzzle stickers on page 33. When you finish, find the object's sticker on page 45 and place it in the secret hideout on page 23.

Blastoff!

The explorers take a sightseeing tour to outer space

in their **rocket ship**.

Ben takes a picture of their space friend.

▶ Use the puzzle stickers on page 35. When you finish, find the object's sticker on page 45 and place it in the secret hideout on page 23.

Emma and Ben find a treasure chest full of jewels! Emma tries on a glittery, sparkling **diamond** ring. She takes a picture of it before returning it to the chest.

▶ Use the puzzle stickers on page 37. When you finish, find the object's sticker on page 45 and place it in the secret hideout on page 23.

At their next destination,

a mighty **dragon** surprises the explorers.

Emma and Ben hide, and then they take a picture of it.

Roar!

▶ Use the puzzle stickers on page 39. When you finish, find the object's sticker on page 45 and place it in the secret hideout on page 23.

9

The explorers come across

a grand **castle**.

They run to the top and wave to everyone below them.

Then they run down to the ground and

take a picture of the castle.

▶ Use the puzzle stickers on page 41. When you finish, find the object's sticker on page 45 and place it in the secret hideout on page 23.

As the explorers travel home,
a **butterfly** flutters by them.

Ben takes a picture of it, and it flies away.

It's almost time for their adventure to end.

▶ Use the puzzle stickers on page 43. When you finish, find the object's sticker on page 45 and place it in the secret hideout on page 23.

Emma and Ben are finally home.

They now have lots of objects to add to

their new **collection** that will

remind them of their adventure.

Memories of Exploration

These are the objects we found on our adventure.

① Apple

② Cake

③ Cheeseburger

④ Panda

⑤ Elephant

⑥ Rocket ship

⑦ Diamond

⑧ Dragon

⑨ Castle

⑩ Butterfly

It was fun!
See you soon!!

Cover design by Meehyun Thompson

Illustrations by NuQ

Supervised by Mogi Kenichiro

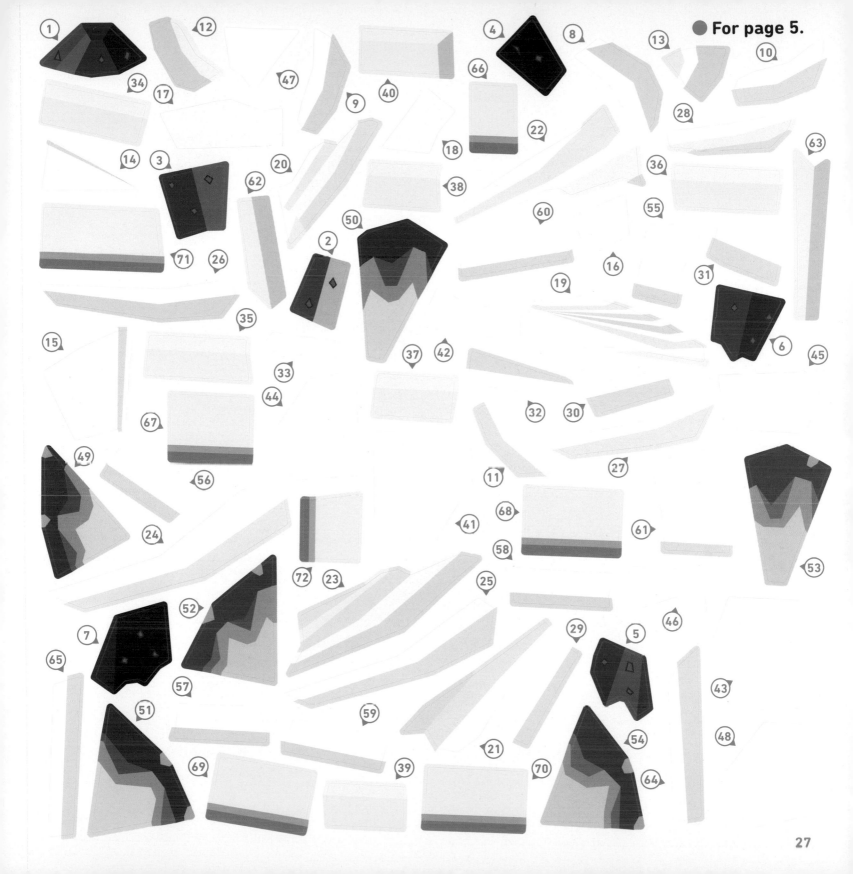

For page 5.

For page 7.

29

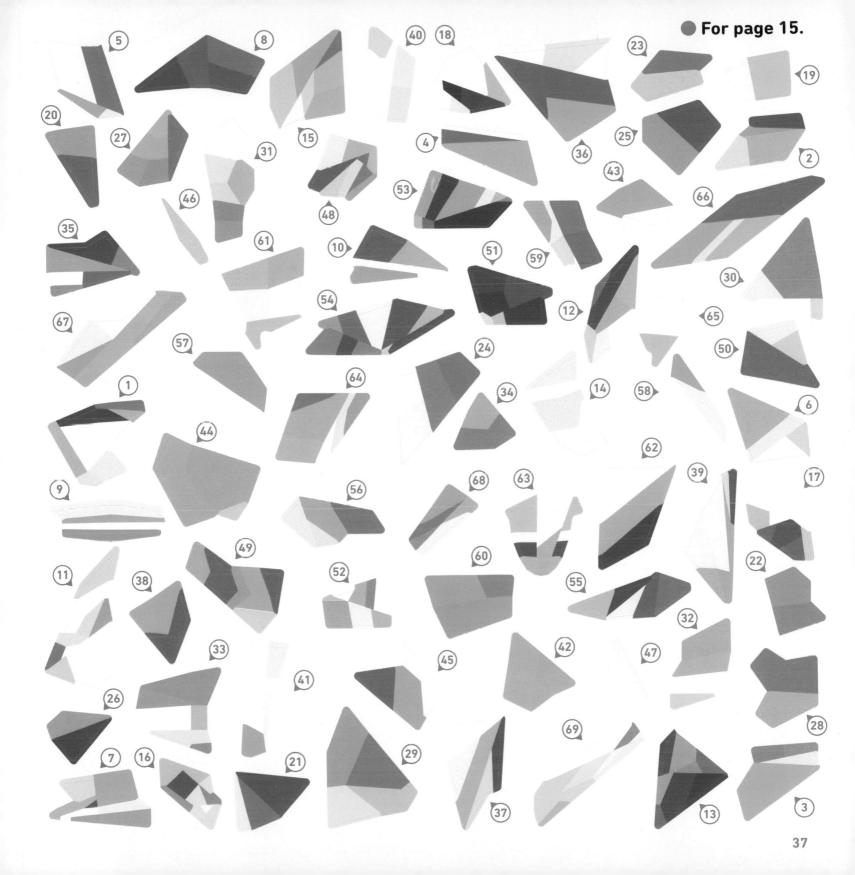

For page 21.

43

COLLECTION STICKERS

Place stickers ① to ⑩ in the secret hideout.
Put the leftover stickers anywhere you want!

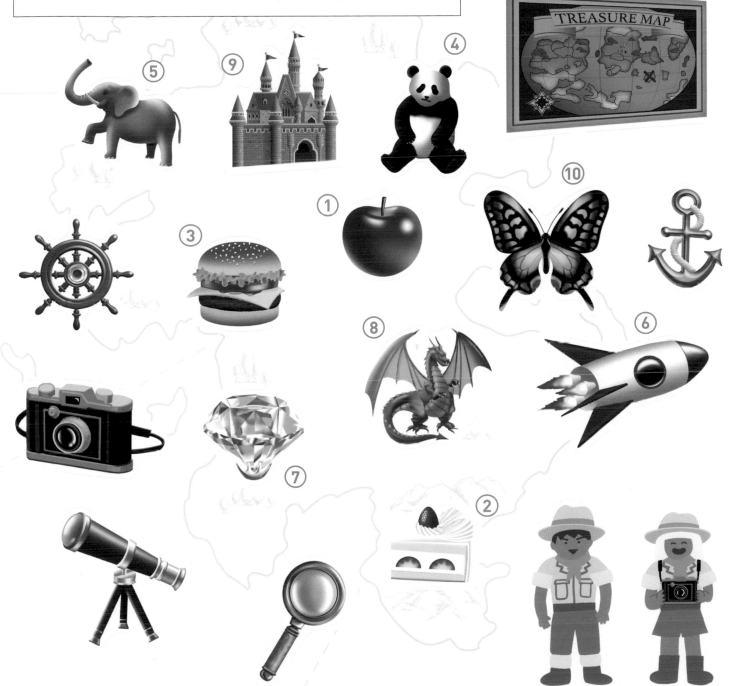